غولْ! هيا نلعبْ!

Goal! Let's Play!

Joe Marriott
Illustrated by Algy Craig Hall

Arabic translation by Wafa' Tarnowska

Mantra Lingua

إسمي تشنْ وأنا ألعبُ الفوتبولَ
كلَ يوم.

I'm Chen and I play football every day.

Thwack

boing

Goal!

Let's score!

إسمي دانيلا. أحبُ لعبَ كرةِ السلةِ
معَ أصدقائي.

My name's Daniella.
I love playing basketball
with my friends.

Boing
phwoop
through the hoop!

Let's shoot!

أنا شيتْ وأحبُ لعبَ البيسبولْ معَ فريقي.

I'm Chet and I love playing baseball with my team.

WHACK WHIZ

LET'S CATCH!

THUNK CAUGHT!

5 4

إسمي فارسْ. أنا وأبي نتسابقُ على
الجمل.

My name's Faris. Daddy and I
are racing on a camel.

Humpety!
Bumpety!
Thumpety!

Let's ride!

أنا كيتي وأُحبُ تطيرَ طيارةِ الورقِ
على رأسِ التلة.

I'm Katy and I fly my kite
at the top of the hill.

Let's fly!

Whoosh!

zoom!

Zip!

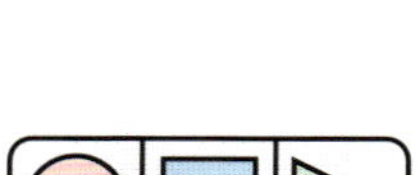

إسمي بيارْ وأنا أَسرَعُ راكضٍ في الصف.

My name's Pierre. I'm the fastest runner in my class.

Huff puff whiz whistle!

Let's race!

أنا ناديا وأُحبُ السباحةَ معَ أَصدقائي في الماءِ المنعش.

I'm Nadia and I love swimming with my friends in the cool water.

splish
splash
sploosh!

Let's dive!

إسمي جيمسْ وأَنا أَلعبُ التنسْ معَ
عائلتي كلَ عطلةِ أخرِ الأسبوع.

My name's James. I play tennis with my family every weekend.

Whack!

Wham!

Boing!

SLAM!

Let's serve!

أنا مارتا و أَنا أتعلمُ لعبةَ الجودوْ في
قاعةِ الرياضة.

I'm Marta and I'm learning judo in the gym.

Spin!

Chop!

Flip!

Flop!

Let's throw!

أنا توماسْ ويمكنني التزلجَ على
الثلجِ بسرعةٍ فائقة.

I'm Tomas and I can
ski really fast.

Swish! Swerve!

Whiiiiiiiiiiiiiiiiizzzzzzzz z z z!

Let's ski!

إسمي نيتشْ و أُحبُ لعبَ الكريكتْ
مَعَ أصدقائي وعائلتي.

My name's Nitesh. I love playing cricket with my friends and family.

Whoooosh!

Thwaaacc c c ckk!

Let's bowl!

Mexico
UK
Nigeria
Switzerland
Dubai
China
Australia
India
Spain
America
France
?
i